The Moment of
Truth

A Worldwide Emergency

Tamara Jackson

Order this book online at www.trafford.com
or email orders@trafford.com

Most Trafford titles are also available at major online book retailers.

Tamara Jackson previously performed for MLK celebration (2008), NAACP celebration (reciting Diaspora), and with Black Poets Ventures (during a black history tribute) she also displays her unique talent in various churches and community venues . . . .

Printed in the United States of America.

ISBN: 978-1-4669-1822-1 (sc)
ISBN: 978-1-4669-1824-5 (hc)
ISBN: 978-1-4669-1823-8 (e)

Library of Congress Control Number: 2012903719

Trafford rev. 03/23/2012

 www.trafford.com

North America & international
toll-free: 1 888 232 4444 (USA & Canada)
phone: 250 383 6864 ♦ fax: 812 355 4082

Contents

Dedication

I would like to dedicate this to the most high God, I first and foremost thank you for instilling in me your truths and directions for this righteous path I take, I also thank you for trusting me with this assignment. I want to trust you in all times and go forth in you and complete all tasks that you have prepared for me, thank you for the many inspirations I met and encountered along the way, and I know you are not through with me yet, and I look forward to more blessings you have for me; you said in your word that we are your children and you will hold no good thing from us, and I stand in agreement with those who believe and in the gap for those who don't, trusting that you will supply their needs of strength, courage, faith, healing (spiritual, mental, emotional, physical, and all) . . . .

I also want to thank all my friends, family, and fans for your support for buying the book or however you were blessed to get and read a copy, and know that it is not by accident that you did, because it is certain that God has something in here for you, but thanks again, I love you and God bless . . . .

Meditation

I felt the obligation to share with you all the wisdom knowledge and understanding God has allowed and permitted me to learn and obtain. This is my ministry and I am delighted that the Lord has chosen me to spread and share it;

"Glory be to God for His mercy and many blessings in my life! Psalms 100 says;

1. Make a joyful noise unto the Lord, all ye lands.

2. Serve the Lord with gladness: come before His presence with singing.

3. Know ye that the Lord He is God: it is He that hath made us, and not we ourselves; we are His people, and the sheep of his pasture.

4. Enter into His gates with thanksgiving, and into His courts with praise: be thankful unto Him, and bless His name.

5. For the Lord is good; His mercy is everlasting; and His truth endureth to all generations.

"I am so excited about this journey; my walk with God and God walking with me: ya see I face many trials that has me to lose focus and become discouraged at times, and though I don't deal oh too well with fear and discourage, but I thank Him for being merciful and allowing us a grace period, time and chances to get back up, to repent, to come back into His presence and confess our faults and our downfalls! I may not be where I suppose to be or where I'm going, but dear God I'm not where I use to be, thanking Him for growth . . . .

As I look around I see evidence more and more each day that the prophecies are being fulfilled (as I've been taught and believe them to be) God is constantly giving me insight and discernment, now I don't claim to know the exact date of the end or return of Christ, but I do know/realize that the things that I witness are true signs that relate to the Holy Bible (KJV, NIV, NLT, ETC.) . . . . I am so excited to write this book for you all, I mean I have written and published other books in the past that I was obviously proud of and excited about, but to know that I'm doing something for the Lord, and helping people, I mean really helping people (life changing and effectively), like a child with her birthday on Christmas, lol . . . .

But I wish you all enjoyment, happiness, and blessings . . . .

Preface

As the word says, we are saved and strengthened by our testimonies, so I will share mine in the hopes/prayers that they will be quite effective to you, I mean my encounters and experiences with people on a daily basis, I mean in grocery stores, on Facebook, and surprisingly at church, that's right at church, prompts me even more to look up and be on watch for the return of the king! Everything does happen for a reason, and the things that's happening in today's world tells me I better get my house in order; what say you???

I was watching an evangelic program earlier and the message was about hatred, that's the true reason why we have so much war in the world, because of hatred, we are so angry at our forefathers and ourselves and we take it out on each other, and honestly though some may not admit it but they're angry at God too, and maybe its because of jealousy, yaw remember satan?, he was jealous of God and he lost his position in heaven, but he wanted it all, he wanted the power, the glory and all, but we must be careful because the power He gives us is the only power we need or should have, ya see sometimes we can be too greedy, you ever heard the expression eyes bigger than the stomach? That is to say greedy, but I don't want my spiritual eyes to be too big for my stomach, that's why I trust in God's word when He say He'll never put more on us than we can bare! After all what God has for me it is for me, and I only want my share, praise God . . . .

Love, Peace, and Soul

First of all my condolence goes out to the family of Don Cornelius.

Don you have in a way done what Jesus has done/is doing for the people, created a platform and way for folks to come from all walks of life, enjoy and live freely; its not a black thing and its not a white thing, but it's a come one come all thing! Don Cornelius in a way imitated Jesus by spreading a message of welcome and love, but in his own way by way of entertainment and opportunity, well Jesus is not in this for entertainment purposes, but He definitely offers a huge opportunity, the opportunity to live and express Love, keep the Peace, and save your Soul . . . .

All Aboard

And speaking of Don Cornelius, a legend who will be greatly missed, he started a movement not just a business, made life changes not just money (obviously), he built pride and esteem not just an empire, but unfortunately we can't have Don Cornelius back nor another one of him, there may be few who can duplicate and imitate him, but as the song says, aint nothing like the real thing baby, but we can have Jesus, He is coming back, even the great Al Green brought that confirmation on the set of Soultrain, this is a train ride you would not want to miss, so in the words of the greatest conductor that ever lived (Jesus Christ) "All Aboard", and it won't stop until it reaches it's Destination, Amen?

What kind of wagon has no wheels?

Back in the summer of 1989 when I graduated from 8th grade, one Friday night I went to church with my friend and her mom, it was a bunch of us (almost half the block of us, kids and all), anyhow when they did the alter call at the end of service my friend's mom suggested that she go up there and she did and then her sister and then 1 by 1 the rest of us followed, well I only went because the others went, and I didn't want to be the outcast/square/secluded but yet included. So after that we all did get baptized and I truly believe because I joined the bandwagon I did it because it was the most popular move since everyone was doing it, it did not work for me, I didn't really understand what was going on, so I did not grow spiritually, can you imagine a little red wagon with no wheels, how far do you think it will go? So to answer the question a wagon with no wheels is a bandwagon and it doesn't support too much weight and carry heavy loads, so don't go for the ride because you like the paint job on it . . . .

Hear ye, Hear ye

Hear ye hear ye o generation of people; Psalms 95 says,

1. O COME, let us sing unto the Lord: let us make a joyful noise to the rock of our salvation.

2. Let us come before His presence with thanksgiving, and make a joyful noise unto Him with Psalms.

3. For the Lord is a great God, and a great King above all gods.

4. In His hand are the deep pieces of the earth: the strength of the hills is His also.

5. The sea is His and He made it: and His hands formed the dry land.

6. O COME, let us worship and bow down: let us kneel before the Lord our maker.

7. For He is our God; and we are the people of His pasture, and the sheep of His hand. Today if ye will hear His voice.

8. Harden not your heart, as in the day of temptation in the wilderness:

9. When your fathers tempted me, proved me, and saw my work.

10. Forty years long was I grieved with this generation, and said, it is a people that err in their heart, and they have not known my ways:

11. Unto whom I swore in my wrath that they should not enter into my rest.

Also take note my fellow people, it is not good to fall into the hands of an angry God, so basically you don't wanna get on His bad side . . . .

Observations

When I look around I see many of things, things that Make my spirit quiver and some things that makes me happy, altogether I pay close attention to the happenings. I told my pastor that when I'm looking like a deer trapped in headlights and it seems like I'm lost, I guess I'm just mesmerized by the truth and real stuff, but I'm actually utilizing my imagination, (parse) I absorb and take it all in because I don't want to miss anything, especially if its what the Lord has for me and wants me to know! I can actually say at times I may be lost in the thought, whereas I'm picturing the circumstance surrounding the message (as I said imagining) or should I say contrasting in my head and in my spirit. Truth be told we all need to do some contrasting, take notes ya know make some observations and hear what the Lord God is saying to us, right? He that has an ear let him hear.

Do you hear what I hear?

You may find it strange but He said we are a peculiar people right? Well find it peculiar that you can hear or discern God's voice and message in lyrics (song) and all around you. Some may think I'm crazy when I say I heard him speak through songs, well not to necessarily say that it was God's voice, but God does work in mysterious ways, doesn't He? I use to listen to rap and one of my all—time favorite artists is Lil Wayne, no not for his looks and his style, but because Lil Wayne is gifted in so many ways, very talented, and he is unique as ever, he is being used by God and probably don't even realize it, but allow me to share a testimony if you will; I was listening to Pastor Mason (Mason Bethea/ ex bad boy)on 101.5 jamz when I stayed in Phoenix, and he aired every Thursday for his show called inspiration Thursdays or something like that, anyway as he shared the details of his encounter with Wayne and his entourage, I was moved and then I thought about Wayne's song (A Millie) or however ya spell it, and I thought about the verse where he says everybody fears me but don't nobody feel me, and instantly my mind was focused on God, about how so many fear Him and what He can do, but not too many people are really feeling Him, if they did would we live in a world like this? So many hearts have waxed cold, look at the lack of respect for the elders, look at the lack of respect for even the law, the other day my fiancé was telling me how he had seen a guy walking around downtown Chicago Smoking marijuana, I mean really? I mean this isn't Gary Indiana; I believe they passed the law there for marijuana use anywhere/publicly even. But I just wanted to point out that if we really listened to things around us (song lyrics, birds chirping, etc.) we can hear God's voice or what He is trying to tell us, oh yea I love Lauren Hill's Zion, but Lady Gaga's Born this way I will not except because I serve a God who can change any situation, circumstance or illness, you may have been born that way but you don't have to live and die that way! Amen?

Its 09-04-12, I was just about to start on a new chapter, but then I had taken me a nap and when I woke up I had to go pick up my girls from girl scouts at this restaurant they went out to eat at, stay with me now, cause in this small segment I'm about to reveal confirmation and coincidence, well since by God everything happens for a reason anyway, as I was driving over to get the girls for some reason in my spirit the word inappropriate stood out, then while I was picking them up from the restaurant there was another saint standing in line ahead of me, and this younger lady was saying some things that I thought were disrespectful to the saint, but when I spoke to the lady/girl, she mentioned that the saint had told her she was being inappropriate. Well if anyone thinks I'm weird about this one then so be it, but I told you I pay attention to everything around me right?

Plus remember how earlier I was discussing how theres an obscene amount of disrespect? I strongly believe God set this up like this, what say you? I know that there are some will not believe, but as for me I do, as I say I stand in agreement for those who believe and I stand in the gap for those who don't, Amen!

God uses whom He chooses

I was just speaking with one of my sisters in Christ and we were discussing our yesterday's service and the confirmation in the message, ya know how usually one has to go through training and such before they can prove their knowledge and authentic love for God? Well the message said that God is raising up people to preach and teach, with authentic zeal and the traditional stuff is bound to cease, because too often congregations, etc. feel that certain people aren't ready because they don't meet their standards or qualifications;

Or like when they say women aren't supposed to be preaching, well isn't that up to God? I know in the word (KJV) it says that a woman should be silent in the church, but does anyone really know what that means? Does that mean that women cannot spread the gospel and truth about God? I mean I'm still learning but someone explain that to me, because I thought that God was/is in control, I mean I'm not a preacher but I have to be real about Jesus and what He has done for me!

Since the beginning of time God has been calling whoever He chooses, to prophesy, teach, bless, etc. He calls children, look at David and Samuel, I mean I look on Youtube today and I see little kids as young as 5 years old praising and worshipping Him, and if that's what gets a person's attention and draws them back to God, you think He'll be against it? Besides the word says unless we are like children or become as children (loving, forgiving, humble, etc.) we cannot inherit the kingdom, correct? Children are a perfect example of how we should and supposed to be, that's why Jesus was so compassionate about them, well He was compassionate for everyone, but I think He had a unique love for the children, because even He was as a child, even when His enemies persecuted Him, and crucified Him; picture 2 kids playing and the one makes the other mad, well before too long those 2 kids will be right back playing again, because they have forgiven each other and buried the hatchet . . . .

Shame on you

This is terrible, I was just watching Judge Mathis and you know how at the end they have the ask the judge a question segment? Well a young lady asked if she could sue a pastor if he stole money from her church, whaaat? Here it is you supposed to teach and preach not to steal and you stealing, you're supposed to teach not to lie and you're lying, you're supposed to teach to be against fornication, adultery, rape, and all that's contrary to God's law, but you're acting like everything but a child of God, correction, you're acting like a child of God in the forefront, pulpit and all, but God has a way of exposing you, look out Bishop Eddie Long, and all. Please don't get me wrong this is not a dis or taunting, but a realization to point out that the saying is definitely true, what is done in the dark will grow sunshine and come to the light, so you can't be too careful with your secrets when you messing with God, its either get right or get out, stop secretly doing dirt and hiding behind the pulpit, titles, God, and thinking He not gone put you out there, afterall where is the respect for Him and His word anyway? As the truth says, God is not mocked and His word does not come back void and unaccomplished . . . .

Excited About Jesus

"I'm excited and I keep singing Send up the war cry by Shekinah Glory, its a song that is sticking in my spirit for some reason, my fiancé just told me how beautifully my eyes are shining, and I just smiled, because I realize it's the Holy Spirit in me or as Mary Mary say, it's the God in me, "Hallelujah". I'm so excited, I'm taking a course called the tabernacle class, which is to teach the reason why church exists, it's original purpose and all, something for the saints of God to better appreciate Him and respect His dwelling more, but not everyone sees it like that, and I have personally witnessed some things in some churches today that makes me go hmmm, but that's another story, and God knew this would be, so He even mentioned in His word how everybody who says Lord Lord will not enter into the kingdom or is not fit for the kingdom of heaven. Anyway I rushed over to class tonight thinking that it was scheduled for tonight, and when I got there it was not, but look how God works mysteriously here, the dean which is the teacher of the class tried to call me to let me know that there was no class, and since I was running a little late I decided to call him and inform him, well needless to say we couldn't reach each other for different reasons, well God had an ulterior motive, ya see it wasn't until I got there when I found out there was no class, but why do you think that we couldn't get in touch with each other? Well, God showed me that if he had reached me or I reach him, he would have been able to stop me from driving all the way over to the church, but God allowed me to make it there and back by faith because I don't have much gas in my car, and my gas hand is broke so I never know when I'm about to run out of gas, which I have plenty of times, and God wanted to see my true zeal, desire, sincere concern, plus He wanted to show it to me anyway, cause He is a God who knows all, and I thank Him because I need some reassurance of myself sometimes, and when God shows me to me, glory, anybody ever pray for the Lord to allow them to see themselves how He does, I'm sure many of you do, and its my daily prayer, and just look at God. And in closing of this testimony, about a week ago I probably would have complained about burning out necessary gas, but God just allowed me to smile and even laugh at the whole situation, and I was just glad that I had that experience, Amen?

Things that make ya go "hmmm"

Remember I just mentioned I have seen some disturbing things in church, I'm not too surprised to see it in the streets but in church or in Holy people? I'm about to step on some toes here, so if its you then you might wanna move your feet (change your ways or as the Bible says, consider your ways) also the Bible says In Isaiah 58 & 59; (58)

1. CRY ALOUD, and spare not, lift up thy voice like a trumpet, and show my people their transgression, and the house of Jacob their sins.

2. Yet they seek me daily, and delight to know my ways, as a nation that did righteousness, and forsook not the ordinance of their God: they ask of me the ordinances of justice they take delight in approaching God.

3. Wherefore have we fasted, say they, and thou seest not? Wherefore we afflicted our soul, and thou takest no knowledge?
   Behold, in the day of your fast ye find pleasure, and exact all your labours.

4. Behold, ye fast for strife and debate, and to smite with the fist of wickedness: ye shall not fast as ye do this day, to make your own voice to be heard on high.

5. It is such a fast that I have chosen? A day for a man to afflict his soul? Is it to bow down his head as a bulrush, and to spread sackcloth and ashes under him? Wilt thou call this a fast, and an acceptable day to the Lord?

6. Is not this the fast that I have chosen? To loose the bands of wickedness, to undo the heavy burdens, and to let the oppressed go free, and that ye break every yoke?

7. Is it not to deal thy bread to the hungry, and that thou bring the poor that are cast out to thy house? When thou seest the naked, that thou cover him; and that thou hide not thyself from thy own flesh?

8. Then shall thy light break forth as the morning and thou health shall spring forth speedily: and thy righteousness shall go before thee: the glory of the Lord shall be thy reward.

9. Then shalt thou call, and the Lord shall answer; thou shalt cry, and He shall say, here I am, If thou take away the midst of thee the yoke, the putting forth of the finger, and speaking vanity;

10. And if thou draw out thy soul to the hungry, and satisfy the afflicted soul; then shall light arise in obscurity, and the darkness be as the noonday:

11. And the Lord shall guide thee continually, and satisfy thy soul in drought, and make fat thy bones: and thou shalt be like a watered garden, and like a spring of water, whose waters fail not.

12. And they that shall be of thee shall build the old waste places: thou shalt raise up the foundations of many generations; and thou shalt be called, The repairer of the breach, The restorer of the paths to dwell in.

13. If thou turn away thy foot from the Sabbath, from doing thy pleasure on my Holy day; and call the Sabbath a delight, the Holy of the Lord,

honourable; and shalt Him, not doing thy own ways, nor finding thine own pleasures, nor speaking thine own words:

14. Then shalt thou delight thyself in the Lord; and I will cause thee to ride upon the high places of the earth, and feed thee with the heritage of Jacob thy father: for the mouth of the Lord hath spoken it. 59

1. Behold, The Lord's hand is not shortened, that it cannot save; neither His ear heavy, that it cannot hear:

2. But your iniquities have separated between you and your God, and your sins have hid His face from you, that He will not hear.

3. For your hands are defiled with blood, and your fingers with iniquity; your lips have spoken lies, your tongue hath muttered perverseness.

4. None calleth for justice, nor any pleadeth for truth: they trust in vanity, and speak lies; they conceive mischief, and bring forth iniquity.

5. They hatch cockatrice' eggs, and weave the spider's web: he that eateth of their eggs dieth, and that which is crushed breaketh out into a viper.

6. Their webs shall not become garments, neither shall they cover themselves with their works of iniquity, and the act of violence is in their hands.

7. Their feet run to evil, and they make haste to shed innocent blood: their thoughts are thoughts of iniquity: wasting and destruction are in their paths.

8. The way of peace they know not; and there is no judgment in their goings: they have made them crooked paths: whosoever goeth therein shall not know peace.

9. Therefore is judgment far from us, neither doth justice overtake us: we wait for light, but behold obscurity; for brightness, but we walk in darkness.

10. We grope for the wall like the blind, and we grope as if we had no eyes: we stumble at noonday as in the night; we are in desolate places as dead men.

11. We roar all like bears, and mourn sore like doves: we look for judgment, but there is none: for salvation, but it is far off from us.

12. For our transgressions are multiplied before thee, and our sins testify against us: for our transgressions are with us: and as for our iniquities, we know them;

13. Transgressing and lying against the Lord, and departing away from our God, speaking oppression and revolt, conceiving and uttering from the heart words of falsehood.

14. And judgment is turned away backward, and justice standeth afar off: for truth is fallen in the street, and equity cannot enter.

15. Yea, truth faileth: and he that departeth from evil maketh himself a prey: and the Lord saw it, and it displeased Him that there was no judgment.

16. And He saw that there was no intercessor: therefore His arm brought salvation unto Him; and His righteousness, it sustained Him.

17. For He put on righteousness as a breastplate, and an helmet of salvation upon His head; and He put on the garments of vengeance for clothing, and was clad with zeal as a cloak.

18. According to their deeds, accordingly He will repay, fury to His adversaries, recompense to His enemies; to the islands He will repay recompense.

19. So shall they fear the name of the Lord from the west, and His glory from the rising sun. When the enemy shall come in like a flood, the Spirit of the Lord shall lift up a standard against him.

20. And the Redeemer shall come to Zion, and unto them that turn away from their transgression in Jacob, saith the Lord.

21. As for me, this is my covenant with them, saith the Lord: My Spirit that is upon thee, and my words which I have put in thy mouth, shall not depart out of thy mouth nor out of the mouth of thy seed, nor out of the mouth of thy seed's seed, saith the Lord from henceforth and forever.

Now the Spirit of the Lord lead me here, and it pointed out many things to me as I wrote. But as the song says, we have to get our house in order, stop playing church yaw, stop playing messenger, and stop playing with people's emotions and lives, especially the quote on quote people of God, (pastors, preachers, false prophets and all). In this one church I use to attend, this one lady would always give me a bad vibe or negative energy and treatment because of her insecurity issues with her husband, but honestly if you're focusing on God you wouldn't be focused on the wrong things, besides my salvation is far too important for that. Anyway folks are fighting in the churches (I witnessed it a couple of times), lying right in the pulpit, cussing in church, whoremongering in church, you name it. Like this one girl who I assume has a ministry online, blatantly says she don't like it when folks have not been in contact with you for so long and when someone dies then they'll come around, she also said that she don't even want them coming around even then, in other words keep it moving. Well I didn't agree with her because if you're a quote on quote Christian, you're supposed to look past that issue of whatever kept them from contacting and socializing or whatever (I mean it could have been just flat out inconvenience/ because naturally if you don't talk to a person you can't possibly know what they're going through) but anyway she was basically telling me she wouldn't forgive them, "OMG" where is the love? Really? The body of Christ needs prayer but those that represent it are truly desperate. If you're Christian then you love (practice unconditionally) and love covers a multitude of sin, hurt, and all, but if you love you will forgive, no doubt about it, if not then call the feds cause theres definitely some counterfeit going on . . . .

Consider your ways!

"Mercy, I know the strong one; Elohim!!! God's people its time we get up and strike the enemy back and with a force, it is time to rebuild His house, Amen? Today's message is from Haggai chapter 1. 1. IN THE second year of Darius the king, in the sixth month, in the first day of the month, came the word of the Lord by Haggai the prophet unto Zerubbabel the son of Shealtiel, governor of Judah, and to Joshua the son of Josedech, the high priest, saying, 2. Thus speaketh the Lord of hosts, saying, This people say, The time is not come, The time that the Lord's house should be built. 3. Then came the word of the Lord by Haggai the prophet saying, 4. It is time for you, O ye, to dwell in your ceiled houses, and this house lie waste? 5. Now therefore thus saith the Lord of hosts; Consider your ways. 6. Ye have sown much, and bring in little; ye eat, but ye have not enough; ye drink, but ye are not filled with drink; ye clothe you, but there is none warm; and he that earneth wages earneth wages to put into a bag with holes. 7. Thus saith the Lord of hosts; Consider your ways. 8. Go up to the mountain, and bring wood, and build the house; and I will take pleasure in it, and I will be glorified, saith the Lord. 9. Ye looked for much, and lo, it came to little; and when ye brought it home, I did blow upon it. Why? Saith the Lord of hosts. Because of mine house that is waste, and ye run every man into his own house. 10. Therefore the heaven over you is stayed from dew, and the earth is stayed from her fruit. 11. And I called for a drought upon the land, and upon the mountains, and upon the corn, and upon the the new wine, and upon the oil, and upon that which the ground bringeth forth, and upon men, and upon cattle, and upon all the labour of the hands. 12. Then Zerubbabel the son of Shealtiel, and Joshua the son of Josedech, the high priest, with all the remnant of the people, obeyed the voice of the Lord their God, and the words of Haggai the prophet, as the Lord their God had sent him, and the people did fear before the Lord.13. Then spake Haggai the Lord's messenger in the Lord's message unto the people, saying I am with you, saith the Lord. 14. And the Lord stirred up the spirit of Zerubbabel the son of Shealtiel, governor of Judah, and the spirit of Joshua the son of Josedech, the high priest, and the spirit of all the remnant of the people; and they came and did work on the house of the Lord of hosts, their God, 15. In the four and twentieth day of the sixth month, in the second year of Darius the king. People, we got to stop slacking when it comes to living and doing this thing, we got to do God's business more, we have to go and rebuild His temple get the attention of His people, all the people that are lost, confused and all, stop judging people because of their differences and all. Consider your ways, do you ever wonder why you go through so many things such as stress, depression, poverty, lack, struggles, drugs, and all sorts of habits? Well, its something you're not doing right before the Lord, we spend more time on our own projects in life than His, we are concerned more with our own issues than what concerns Him and His kingdom, why are our houses so disturbed and His house is in waste? Speaking of waste I heard a woman telling the story of a saint who had a dream one time of two trash bags being left on his property and this dream troubled him for some reason, and when he awoke, he said to himself that he had gotten rid of the trash, the waste, (but that was in the natural sense) which means he had taken out his garbage out, but the trash bags in his dream/vision represented his spiritual sense, there were some things in his spiritual life that he had to get rid of (says God) of course he thought he was all good, many of us think we're all good, but God sees what we can't, He knows what we don't and He goes and takes us where we could never even imagine, that's why its good to focus and rely on Him, and also as the word says that we should not lean unto our own understanding, lets learn to express more patience and love, and be not so discriminative to others nor what is right or to people that are not 100% right, we tend to judge others because they are not on our levels, but we must let God do His job, and we do our's . . . .

You Are Not Alone

You are not alone when you praise Him, you are not alone when you face struggles and trials, you are not alone when you're desperate, no you are not alone when Jesus is in your life, and truth be told when Jesus is in your life and when He shows up you better believe that satan will too. When you are doing good, (satan) shows up to turn that thing around just as sure as he is a liar, and everybody knows he is a liar, anyway tonight the pastor of my church wife (first lady) is hosting the council at another church, so we're visiting, and I wanted to go and represent her and support her, now all day I been feeling super excellent and extra excited about Jesus, remember I just wrote earlier about it, but anyhow, I was going to be on time with how I had planned to do things, but all came tumbling down like dominos, from deciding what to wear, my child got me running late, you name it and before you know it I've lost the desire to go because I don't want to show up too late, and by the time we make it to where its located, it might have been over, so I just gave up altogether, but thank God and if its His will I'll try it again tomorrow, but I was not surprised I admit I did have a short tantrum but before it got away from me too far, I caught myself realizing its another trick of the enemy to attempt to still my joy, but we all know that satan is a what? That's right a liar. I use to always wonder why I could not get from God what others had and I mean I would sit under the teachings and could never get it, so I would cry and pray and fast but for some reason it just wouldn't come, but it had to take God to use a certain situation and issue in my life to point out to me the reason and how to deal with it, and eventually I changed, well God changed me, but when God showed myself to me it happened. Remember I told you that I ask God to allow me to see myself the way He sees me, well I didn't realize that was good and bad, which means He showed me the areas I needed work in and needed to change and when I was sincere with Him and confessed/admitted those things, He said now. I had to tell God I have these problems with anger, emotions, controlling, fear, doubt, insecurity and all, and God being an all knowing God, I'm sure He already knew this about me, but He wanted to hear me confess, to see myself the way He did, oh and which turned out to be a good thing altogether and not bad at all, because He used it to help me change! But if/when you find yourself lost, crying, discouraged, confused, hopeless, etc. and if you don't have God in your life or if you struggle with fear, worry, or doubt, just remember you are not alone, and God wants you to rely on Him and confess to Him, and He will show you for sure that you are not alone . . . .

Is He well pleased?

Pride goeth before destruction and an haughty spirit before a fall. (Proverbs 16:18) . . . .

This is for the many people who thinks that them being prideful and turning up their noses is okay with God, well, you're wrong, God doesn't like a boasting man (person) I mean all in the church and out in the world, and again it is somewhat expected and accepted from those in the world but those that are in the church, or should I say those that know better, "wow" as I sit here and watch these televangelist programs I learn, and agree, yes the church today is so different, but God is still the same as yesterday, today and forever more, He changes not, why do people, but ohh I got it, it's the pride of man/mankind, because he thinks he is right, even over God obviously (no not all people are like this). I was watching Joyce Meyers earlier and yes I love her, but like she was saying imagine how the body of Christ would be if Lutheran, Catholics, Baptists, Pentecostal and all were to unite and on one accord, considering not their own doctrine, but the law of the Lord, which is to love, imagine how it would be, but because of pride our world is so confused and corrupt, but the greatest of all is love, as the word says, love covers a multitude of sin, hurt, disrespect, and all. With pure love you wouldn't be able to judge or dislike a person because he is not like you or 100% in agreement with you, there are some of us who say I'm saved and I'm Christian but I don't like him, or I can't stand her, or I won't share, etc. But honestly ask yourself, do you think God is proud of your behavior, I just read last week how even if you speak in tongues, pray, good deeds and all, it means nothing if you don't have charity/love, the Bible says you sound like hallow brass, and that's annoying, do you want to sound or be annoying to God? If you are annoying to God, how then can you be pleasing Him?

Strange Things

I wasn't too sure how I would introduce this chapter to you as well as explain it to you, but the Holy Spirit reminded me and created an instant replay in my mind when I think about the things the Lord did through me and how He brought me through! Like one year I had come to repentance, and was saved (Salvation/sin free). But anyway, I had a dream that I was at a church and during an alter call or something, and I started speaking in tongues, something I hadn't done in a while, being is that I had backslidden, and that next morning (which was Sunday) when I had visited this church and like in my dream at alter call I was filled with the Holy Spirit and began speaking in tongues, I was shocked but I've seen stranger things, like when I was about 6 or 7 years old and my family was having a gathering (picnic) or should I say barbeque. And it had started to rain and my grandmother grabbed me by my hand and ran underneath the shed in our backyard, as we ran I dropped my teddy bear or whatever toy it was, and by the time we made it to the shed it seemed to be pouring down, but my grandmother stepped out from under the shed to get my toy and when she did it immediately stopped raining, almost like the day had just dried up altogether. And when she stepped back underneath the shed, it instantly started back pouring rain even harder than before, what just went on, I'm sure everybody wondered, but even as a child I just knew it was God.

Tamara Jackson

One day while I was living in Phoenix Az. I visited church with pastor Mason, and at the end of service they opened up the doors (meaning they welcomed folks to come forth if they want to receive salvation) however they did that and when I spoke with Twyla (Mason's wife)I shared with her about my anxiety, depression, and all other problems I was dealing with, and she immediately pulled me to the side/backstage, where she began laying hands on me and praying, she then called for a few more men (Elder, Pastor, etc.) all I remembered is my body slinging and panting, as the voices moaned and snarled and huffed and puffed as they gasped for air, that's right you guessed it, they were rebuking or casting demons/devils out of me, but they were resisting at first, in a sense mocking Jesus I guess, and speaking of mocking a few years before that while I was living down there also, my ex mother by law had a few of her church buddies over and the man of the 3 laid hands on me, but it wasn't like anything I had ever experienced or felt before, but my body was limp as I sat in a chair, and the more he compelled the demons to come out, the more they laughed, I mean it was crazy, I couldn't do anything but lay there, sitting up straight with my head leaned back and an uncontrollable laughter coming from me? I thought. But you know how they say be careful of who you let put their hands on you, and I'm not sure how to do that anyway, well today I can say I am sure glad to have on my side a God that can protect you from all harm, but I heard that man used to worship the devil, and then shortly after that encounter with me, he went back to it.

Another time I was standing in my kitchen and I had poured me a cup of coffee and right when I was stirring it, I was taken by the thought/vision, I seen myself falling out, and then I thought to myself what if? And after that the rest was a shocking history, I'm not sure if I was doing something wrong or disappointing to the Holy Spirit, but to this day I say, God tapped me and knocked me out, now I'm sure if He had used any more force it wouldn't have been as simple and light, anyway I suddenly fell/passed out, dropping to the floor instantly and without the ability to even break my fall, anyhow I ended up bumping my head on the wall (brick wall mind you) and after about a minute I woke up and noticed coffee all over my floor, and what convinced me that I had passed out or fainted or something was that when I became conscious, before I got up from the floor and even before I opened my eyes, I felt and heard myself snoring, what was that? I thought to myself, but my wise and common sense told me not to even question that. We (my kids and I) would go to Bible studies on Wednesdays, and one night I had, and during the course of the study, we would watch a movie and a little portion of prayer and then we would do questions, and sometimes that meant testimonies, confessions and more, this particular night as they prayed for me and over me, the Holy Spirit's Presence was strong in me, that a force took over me causing me to pitch my voice (almost like singing but without a melody) in this high tone, seemingly angelic, like an angel sounding her trumpet, I mean even to this day I wonder what was happening and why, but we can't question God's purpose for us . . . .

Trust and Believe

The number one thing is to Trust and Believe, there are so many scriptures that support and surround Trust and Believe;

Job 13:15 Though He slay me, yet will I trust in Him: but I will maintain mine own ways before Him. Psalms 25:2 O my God, I trust in thee: let me not be ashamed, let not mine enemies triumph over me.

Psalms 37:3 Trust in the Lord, and do good; so shalt thou dwell in the land, and verily thou shalt be fed. Psalms 143:8 Cause me to hear thy lovingkindness in the morning; for in thee I trust: cause me to know the way wherein I should walk: for I lift up my soul unto thee.

Proverbs 3:5 Trust in the Lord with all thine heart; and lean not unto thine own understanding. Isaiah 50:10 Who is among you that feareth the Lord, that obeyeth the voice of his servant, that walketh in darkness, and hath no light? Let him trust in the name of the Lord, and stay upon his God. Matthew 27:43 He trusted in God; let him deliver him now, and if he will have him: for he said I am the son of God. (Even though this particular verse was when they made mockery of Jesus, but because He did trust in the Lord despite their foolishness, He was lifted up into glory and was declared the son of man) . . . .

Mark 11:24 Therefore I say unto you, what things soever ye desire, when ye pray, believe that ye receive them. Luke 8:13 They on the rock are they, which, when they hear, receive the word with joy: and these have no root, which for a while believe, and in the time of temptation fall away. John 1:12 But as many as received Him, to them gave he power to become the sons of God, even to them that believe on His name. John 11:26 And whosoever liveth and believeth in me shall never die, Believest thou this? John 14:1 Let not your heart be troubled; ye believe in God, believe also in me. Acts 16:31 And they said, Believe on the Lord Jesus Christ, and thou shalt be saved, and thy house.

Romans 9:33 As it is written, Behold, I lay in Si'-on a stumblingstone and rock of offense: and whosoever believeth on Him shall not be ashamed. Romans 10:14 How then shall they call on Him in whom they have not believed? Galatians 3:22 But the scripture hath concluded all under sin, that the promise by faith of Jesus Christ might be given to them that believe. 2 Timothy 1:12 For the which cause I also suffer these things: nevertheless I am not ashamed: for I know whom I have believed, and am persuaded that He is able to keep that which I have committed unto him against that day. Hebrews 11:6 But without faith it is impossible to please Him: for he that cometh to God must believe that He is, and that He is a rewarder of them that diligently seek Him.

James 2:19 Thou believest that there is one God; thou doest well: the devils also believe, and tremble.

These scriptures and many more has helped me and still helps me to grow, believing and trusting in God I was able to get over a lot of my fears, I was able to get over a lot of hurt and pain, I was able to endure a lot of things and issues and situations, I trusted that God will be with me, that He will comfort me, that He will bring me out no matter what it is, now I refuse to act like I'm perfect or that I'm superwoman, but I still struggle with some things, I still face certain circumstances, I still face and am confronted by fear from time to time, but without doubt when I take it to His throne (the throne of mercy and grace) I can overcome, and of course that comes by trusting and believing!

My Testimony

Good God morning yaw, I feel good today, well I feel good everyday that the good Lord wakes me up, and ya know I gotta be feeling good cause by gracious God I'm not dead yet, Amen? Anyway I got a super breakthrough yesterday, and just as my pastor said and I know it to be true, whenever you hear from God or He elevates His presence in your life or whatever, the devil is sure to come in and try to destroy it, create confusion and conflict and all. I confess that I got quite out of my body yesterday at dinner, me and my fiancé gathered our family members and went out after church, and the way I hadn't acted since I was saved, surfaced and cut up, I mean in hindsight I really felt bad because I know that's not suppose be part of my character, but what I want and try to get folks to understand just because you become saved it doesn't mean you are perfect, the power of the Holy Ghost will help you deter from sin (or turn from) but only if you let it, cause if you ignore it and it will after a while ignore you and let you do your thang, which is a dangerous thing, but because God is merciful and has grace for us, He gives us room and time to repent. But anyway I didn't cuss no one out or anything, I was just what they call got real ghetto, as some would say belligerent, but the devil wants me to display such a character, that's why I feel so bad because I let him win. Do you know when I went to pray earlier and while on my knees I felt so bad as God reminded me of yesterday, and though I repented I still felt guilty and shame (hmm, wonder why that was)? Then something came over me and a small voice in the form of a thought (perhaps) said to my mind until you do right by me, meaning I have to live this thing even more seriously than I have been. What do you suppose that was? Well I'm in no position to lie on my God, nor will I ever be, but that's what I got in my spirit . . . . Last night I was watching Phat Girls (Monique), and I noticed how Jasmine (Monique) had dreamed earlier in the movie that she was carried out to the stage or whatever by some masculine attractive men as a queen, and she after going on her trip and finding that security that she was seeking and afraid to face, she came into her identity, happiness, wealth, and then her dream came true, she launched her clothing line, and like she also dreamed she was carried onto the stage at the fashion show by true enough the masculine men, upon her pedastal, and she was happy, she had arrived somewhere, now as Christians I do not think you arrive to a particular place and stay and think its over because God is always taking you to another level, Amen? But you feel the shifting no doubt, my pastor was preaching on yesterday about dreams, and how sometimes your dream can be bigger than your resources, but Monique/Jasmine Biltmore got to the point to where she did not allow her lack of resources keep her from her dream, remember when she tried to get the loan from the bank and they refused her?

Well that didn't stop her, and my testimony is that I can relate, I too had a dream that I was on the Oprah show, I was on the Monique show, I was on Lift Every Voice with Coco brother Corey, I mean I was all over the place and I'm not gonna stop until the dreams come true, and be it God's will it will come to pass.

I use to hold on to the thought of my past from when my uncle touched me (molested), which created a mental disease for me and caused me to be in psychiatric treatment and all, from all my abusive relationships, from my poverty filled childhood, from my scars and lack of self esteem and allowed that to dictate who I am as a person, for too long I considered myself a failure, I thought I was a loser, I was worthless and hopeless, but God, can somebody say but God? But God, He heard my cries, He heard my prayers on high and He answered, I'm sure that many can agree with me, many of us pray and ask God to allow us to see ourselves the way He sees us, well as they say be careful of what you pray for, well God allowed me to see this very saying differently, which means to be full of care when you pray, you're sincere and therefore He can answer you and in a way that there will be no doubt in your mind. And guess what when I started to realize that I saw exactly what God wanted me to see, because God allowed me to see myself as He sees me, and not just the blessings and the all good part of me, but God showed me the areas I needed work in and all, so that meant the good and the bad, so we know that God is an all seeing God, so He sees more than just the good, but the bad and the troubled also, Amen?

I was just talking to a friend of mine and I mentioned how I'm always inviting her to visit my church but she never comes, she would just tell me shes coming one day, okay now I'm not the one to force anything on anyone, but sometimes about some things we must be consistent, so I bring it up to her again after months of me mentioning it to her the last time, and she tells me that she will be there and that shes trying to get her stuff together, well I don't know how much stuff she got but Jesus said cast your burden on me (Him) He will carry your heavy load, lol, naw but seriously you/we could never get it right without God, beside Hes the one to make it all right for us, people come to church to get that healing for whatever they're going through, ya can't wait thinking you gotta get it right first, don't you know you will be searching for solutions and answers forever, I told my kids and a few others, if you don't want arthritis you better stop running from the wrong things, arthritis is bad enough in your joints and knees and all but to have arthritis in your spirit, you better rub some Jesus on it, this just in; you may use Icy Hot for your joints but Jesus works better and not like watered down Icy Hot, in fact He is just hot because He is not lukewarm, for He will spew you out, Amen? I agree with my friend about getting stuff together, but don't put it off and wait until you get to church, but yes even us saints got some stuff we need to get together.

Epiphanies

"I know that there are many of us at many of times hope and envision things the way they should be and the way that we want them to be, such as plans and all, but when you see it the way God wants you to see it, especially when you ask Him to show you, you see things so clearly and sensibly, and sometimes it takes the weirdest things to happen for God to point out to you whats the what and get your attention, remember the word says whats foolish to men is wisdom of God, we may see things and say that don't make a lot of sense, but God, say it loud, but God, ya see His thoughts are our thoughts. "I'm sitting here watching BET 106 & Park (honoring Whitney Houston) and the first video was Greatest Love of All! And me being me I immediately thought about The Greatest Love Of All being God, and when she says look inside yourself, well He instantly reminded me of my book I wrote (Let Sheedom Ring) and in it I have a poem I wrote which is about looking inside ourselves and finding happiness within ourselves before we could find it in anyone else;

When you think about it God lives inside of you, and He is the greatest love of all, for the Bible says that there is no greater love than this that a man lay down His life, and Jesus and God is one, Amen? I did an article a while ago on Spiritually Raw (an online radio show) and my article was titled Spiritual Awareness + Happiness =

Success, meaning if you find yourself and discover who you are and whose you are, you find happiness, and when you have found happiness you become successful, (in your personal life, your spiritual life, physically, mentally, emotionally and all) success does not only come in the form of fortune and fame . . . .

I'm gonna just let God line things up and work them out for me, what say you? They showed the clip from last year's gospel celebration of Whitney Houston and Kim Burell performing I look to you (God) great choice; "I love you Whitney", as the Bible say mourn with those who mourn, and blessed are they who mourn for they will be comforted, there is plenty room and hope in our God, Amen?

Take My Advice

I just wanted to share a few things, rather pieces of advice, which helped me in the past and are helping me to grow even today, and these golden rules are not only Christianity but for the unsaved as well, just as the word of the Lord says God reigns/rains on the just and the unjust, that's if you're righteous or unrighteous, His love is unconditional and His love is limitless its just that you would be much better off on the right side of the fence, Amen? I don't want no hell hound on my trail, lol, but anyway

1. You do unto others as you want and will have done unto you; (you can't go around treating people wrong and taking advantage of them just because). I mean people have kind hearts and sometimes they just wanna be nice and sharing, but the greedy will eat that up and come back for refill after refill over and over again, but be not deceived, God is not mocked, He sees all and each will get his just deserves.

2. Judge not lest ye be judged, and with the measure you use you will also be judged.(I learned that when you point the finger there is always at least three pointing back at you, so don't be so quick to blame others, and judge them for anything).

3. Don't always walk around shaking a cup, expecting to get something in return when you do good, God is good to you why can't you do it for others?

4. Always put God first in everything you do, and be careful to give Him all the glory, honor, praise and credit, because anything that is done

even by good deed is no good of our own, but God Himself, and without Him we can do nothing.

5. Romans 12: 9-10; 9. Let love be without dissimulation. Ahbor that which is evil; cleave to that which is good. 10. Be kindly affectioned to one another with brotherly love in honour preferring one another. (NLT),

12:9; 9. Don't just pretend to love others. Really love them. Hate what is wrong. Hold on tightly to what is good. (KJV). The Bible says love thy neighbor as thyself, and I use to think that meant next door and on my block, well news flash people, all that are not you yourselves, if you are not joined at the hip you my friend have got to get a grip, love, love, love, believe it or not but that's what we're missing the most here on this earth, that's the cause of so much widespread violence and all, if people loved enough they would spread the love even by respect and influence, in Dionne Warwick's famous words, reach out and touch someone's hand and make this world a better place because you can, shake a hand make a friend, you all feel me don't you? (Lets love one another, because really it shouldn't be money or power or anything else but love that makes the world go around)!!!

They can't prevail

I am honored to see Wendy Williams as she shares her deepest inner secret, as she just disclosed, she is now 15 years clean of smoking crack, that is what she made mention of what she and Whitney had in common, I am privileged to witness her expressing courage in such a way, because that took courage to admit that, but just as I am deeply moved by her testimony, I deeply and sincerely commend her on her accomplishments, I would have never guessed what she shared tonight, as the word says we are overcome and strengthened by our testimonies, I take my wig off to you Wendy, lol, but seriously God has blessed you mightily, and hearing of all the testimonies and things about Whitney and her involvement in the many lives she impacted, she too was blessed as well a blessing. But Wendy look at you now, love you girl and keep your head up!

You know we all have some secrets and things in our lives that can hinder us and keep us from our blessings (such as drug abuse, alcoholism, mental incapability and all) but when you recognize and realize the power of God, oh those obstacles will crumble as dust in the sea, demons and all have to bow, and no they can't prevail . . . .

Praise God for the people who have overcome personal issues such as drug abuse, alcoholism, sexual abuse, prostitution, gang banging/members, smoking (marijuana and tobacco), over eating, over weight, bulimia, or any habit aka demons, God is a healer and He has healed many, but when

He brings you out be careful not to look down on others because of their struggle with abuse or any sickness, but pray for them and keep in mind that that was once you, Amen? Just like there is a reason for every season, there is a demon for every ill thing, depression, cancer, HIV, poverty and all, but in Jesus name they will not prevail!

Unbelievable

This chapter I must say is weird, remember what I said earlier about weird?

It is so unbelievable and weird its almost scary (but God doesn't give us the spirit of fear right)? Anyway remember how I was just talking about epiphanies, this is still the night of 02-13-12 its approximately 12:50 midnight, and I'm up late working on this book, when the Lord gave me this to include, I'm watching BET again, well still because for whatever reason my tv has been glued to this channel all day, anyway, the movie Cinderella is on and Whitney Houston which I had forgot, is the fairy God mother to Cinderella (played by Brandi) and they're speaking about dreams, remember I mentioned dreams earlier? The weird thing is I just wrote the presentation for the concept I'm working on, The Magnificent Ball (Cinderella The Saint) a stage play I wrote that was given to me by God. I experience weird things a lot, almost daily and this is how God gets my attention, and I have to speak on it, so if anyone thinks I'm crazy for doing so, well, they must take it to God but I have to be obedient, God don't give us things to be silent and shut in a corner, He says let your light shine, even if its dim to some others, right?

Dedicated is not overrated

"I will bless the Lord, o my soul, and all that is within me" "my God how I am so excited, I was just singing a song that one of the sisters made up and had the congregation singing along with her, she said something I'm sure very many can relate to, and that is when the Lord brings you through some things and blesses you, no matter what that situation may be, if you are truly moved, excited, and love Him, you find yourself even making up songs for Him, and the song she made up goes like this, "I feel a praise, I feel a praise, I feel a praise, "Hallelujah", oh how I wish people can sing along with me, I mean that sister had us all jumping, and I give a special shout out to sister Angela Abrams, girl you bring such exuberance to the atmosphere, and I know your trying times but no one can tell, this is evidence of how God is indeed blessing you, Amen? "I love you girly!

I wanted to share with you the assignment given in new members class, at my church, which was to find words or thoughts from A to Z that describe God in my own words, and this is what I came up with and yes it's a unique concept, so if anything seem strange it is excused by God!

A-Amazing, B-Brilliant, C-Comforting, D-Dedicated, E-Everlasting, F-Faithful, G-Graceful, H-Honorable, I-Incredible, J-Joyful, K-Kindhearted, L-Loyal, M-Magnificent, N-Noble, O-One and only, P-Precious, Q-Quite the blast, R-Refreshing, S-Special,

T-Trustworthy, U-Unbelievable, W-Winner, X-Xtremely Good,

Y-You are Awesome, Z-Zealous . . . .

> This was a cool assignment and I had fun despite the challenges
> I faced with some of the letters and words, I wasn't sure if others
> would agree with me as far as using my own expressions, but God
> loves uniqueness, that's why He made us all in our own unique
> way, smile . . . .

Believe it or not God really does work in mysterious ways, as my pastor
preached the other day, he mentioned in his sermon what was definitely
confirmation to me, he said you are God's Choice, and I felt compelled to
share it; theres a poem I wrote not long after I started new members class
and the more someone mentions something that relates to it, I feel God's
presence and purpose in my life even more, and even a reason for this
poem, which was even given by Him that sits on high, Amen?

Choices by Tamara Jackson

Relating to the scriptures more daily as I read God gives me what I need,

to keep me pressing forward and eager to succeed;

I can recall my past like yesterday's pain, but I got to go further in the Lord

theres so much more for me to gain;

You have loosened emotional hinges in me like an open door, now I'm

begging you to come in and fill me with more;

I want to please you Lord and be the best that I can be, acceptable in Your

sight when the world is too blind to see;

I can now go through the tests and trials that's usually hard for me to take,

but I'm willing to suffer it all Lord just for Your name's sake;

You are the one whom I adore the one that I admire, and I thank You Lord

for filling me with true fire and desire;

Each time that I'm tested Lord it draws me closer to You, praise Your name

for healing cause healing is what You do;

You mend my broken heart and You dry up all my tears, I thank You Lord for Your comfort You supplied through all the years;

No one can hold me like You can no one else has such encouraging words, the heathens offers speeches that cuts as deep as swords;

But You are so full of love Lord and love is what love does, You love me despite my faults and failures You love me just because;

Well, I too have a crush Lord, "no, I'm in love with You, I love You for all You've done and for choosing me just for You! Amen.

"Thank you Jesus"

Warnings

God sends His people warnings and since we all are God's children we all should take heed right? Like I once said, theres a difference between claiming to be a child of God's and doing His work/business. Yes He is the creator of all, but do you serve Him, I can admit I myself was not always on this path and serving Him the way that I should or could, but when you desire to do His will, oh its something else! But anyway God sends warnings to His people, and His people are those that will listen, obey, and take heed; as per our last night's Bible class spoke about warnings, coming from the book of Amos 6:1-14; 1. Woe to them that are at ease in Zion, and trust in the mountain of Samaria, which are named chief of the nations, to whom the house of Israel came! 2. Pass ye unto Cal'neh, and see; and from thence go ye to Ha'math the great: then go down to Gath of the Phi-lis'tines: be they better than these kingdoms? Or their border better than your border? 3. Ye that put far away the evil day, and cause the seat of violence to come near; 4. That lie upon beds of ivory, and stretch themselves upon their couches, and eat the lambs out of the flock, and the calves out of the midst of the stall; 5. That chant to the sound of the viol, and invent to themselves instruments of music, like David; 6. That drink wine in bowls, and anoint themselves with the chief ointments: but they are not grieved for the affliction of Joseph. 7. Therefore now shall they go captive with the first that go captive, and the banquet of them that stretched themselves shall be removed. 8. The Lord God hath sworn by Himself, saith the Lord the God of hosts, I abhor the excellency of

Jacob, and hate his palaces: therefore I will deliver up the city with all that is therein. 9. And it shall come to pass, if there remain ten men in one house, that they shall die. 10. And a man's uncle shall take him up, and he that burneth him, to bring out the bones out of the house, and shall say unto him that is by the sides of the house, Is there yet any with thee? And he shall say, No. Then shall he say hold thy tongue: for we shall not make mention of the name of the Lord. 11. For behold, the Lord commandeth, and He will smite the great house with breaches, and the little house with clefts. 12. Shall horses run upon the rock? Will one plow there with oxen? For ye have turned judgment into gall, and the fruit of righteousness into hemlock: 13. Ye which rejoice in a thing of nought, which say, Have we not taken to us horns by our own strength? 14. But, behold, I will raise up against you a nation, O house of Israel, saith the Lord the God of hosts; and they shall afflict you from the entering of He'-math unto the river of the wilderness.

Simply put people, we can't go around thinking we got it made just because we are saved, which of course is a good thing, it is the beginning of salvation, but as God/Jesus commanded, we have a work to do, we can't get too relaxed and say I don't have time to be about my Father's business, we be so comfortable that we forget to share a good word with someone, we forget to love, we forget to think of anyone else other than ourselves, you get saved and pass it on, "Zion we are the church", and the church must live, must grow, must go on, not sit up and supposed to be Holy people turning up their noses and looking down on others because of appearance, differences or anything. Arrogance will get you in trouble, and as Jesus said to Peter

"upon this rock I'll build my church and the gates of hell shall not prevail, Peter was strong, that rock that will stand, and we have to be not afraid to take the torch when it is passed to us and pass it on and on and on, but we have to start somewhere, we regularly should not be in a comfort zone, and that simply means as I say never think you have arrived, you still have work to do, and our only comfort zone should be in Jesus to know that He will protect, provide, comfort, and love us, that's security I can always live with and look forward to, but we have even gotten comfortable with degradation, I mean in some of this music (gospel and all) doesn't have God or any positivity in it at all, but I must not rather we must not get so relaxed, and go on about our own lives and business and say the time is not now, look at what happened in the days of Haggai the prophet and king Darius, let God's house lie waste and He will see to it that your house goes to waste . . . .

We have got to be careful here in America, actually in all the world for that matter, but considering America, for one with this new world order stuff, they talking about taking the slogan In God We Trust off of the money, "whaaat? That's probably the last thing we got that's saving us from His wrath, because as I look around and see all this other mess that is angering Him, same sex marriages, disrespect, lack of love, hardened hearts of many, greed, and all, for me the question is no longer, what is this world coming to? But When Lord, when are You coming back? Because as the Bible tells us that when we see these things (signs) know that time is even at hand, be watchful and watch carefully, Amen?

Here goes another one of my moments, my prophetic moments (parse) But yesterday before I went to Bible class and learned about warnings, I had a witness come by my house and she gave me a pamphlet and it was titled and about Armageddon, and she asked what is was or was I familiar with it?

Well be it God's will, I would like to explain it from the Jehovah witness's point of view and do analysis and show comparison, if I can;

ARMAGEDDON WHAT DO SOME SAY IT IS?

"And they assembled them at the place that in Hebrew is called Armageddon"—Revelation 16:6 (English Standard Version).

WHAT do you think of when you hear the word Armageddon"? Likely, images of a major catastrophe spring to mind. Although the word appears only once in the Bible, the term is repeated often by the news media and other religious leaders.

Do popular concepts of Armageddon match what the Bible teaches? The answer is worth knowing. Why? Because the truth about Armageddon can free you from needless fear, brighten your outlook on the future, and influence the way you think about God. Consider the three following questions, and compare popular concepts of Armageddon with what the Bible really teaches.

The Moment Of Truth!

1. Is Armageddon A Man Made Disaster?
2. Is Armageddon A Natural Disaster?
3. Does God Destroy The Earth at Armageddon?

The Truth About **Armageddon:** The watchtower reads; "Demonic spirits . . . go abroad to the kings of the whole world . . . , and they assemble them in the place that in Hebrew is called Harmageddon". (Revelation 16:14) . . .

The KJV reads; For they are the spirits of devils, working miracles, which go forth unto the kings of the earth and of the whole world, to gather them to the battle of that great day of God Almighty. (Revelation 16:14)

Regardless of what exactly we're taught and how we're taught it, one thing is for sure, there will be an end to life as we currently know it and how God chooses to protect and sustain us is totally up to Him, God knows that there is a huge controversy among men, because of religious views, etc.

(He is not a fool) and He is more clever than we could ever imagine, so if you believe in your heart that you are serving Him right, He too has a plan for you, Everyone was taught differently regarding religion, etc. but God is God, yes He is a spirit and He spoke to the seven churches, and He knows that not everyone will agree on the same thing, but be not foolish and disbelieve in Him altogether, what may work for some may not work for others, but I sincerely pray that whatever it is, that His will be done, and I can't wait until all the controversy for religion and all is done away with, because it really bothers me how we write each other off because we are not the same in culture, ethnicity, belief, religion, practice, faith, etc. Jesus is love and the Christian value is the essence of love, and you can be Christ like regardless of your practice of faith or belief, because as I learned long ago Christianity is not a religion but a reality, Jesus is real to me, that's why I feel so confident in the Lord what I say and how I feel, to God be the glory! I have a muslim on the right side for my neighbor, a Baptist directly across the street from me, a church going lady on the left side of me (and I'm not sure of what her religion or faith is) but I know she is my neighbor (she is not myself), and there are countless of people out there in this world who don't even believe in God (I pray for them, because it is obvious that they know not what they do), but I love them all, as God says; love thy neighbor, Amen?

A Devine Tribute & Revelation

Now this may trip some of you out, because it did me, now this is gonna take an intelligent mind to comprehend it's significance, rather you believe or not I want you to line it all up, okay? And do know that God is God, and He is able to do anything, Amen?

Anyway I got an email yesterday to invite me to give a tribute to Whitney Houston (yaw pay attention, because as I said God works in mysterious ways) Guideposts "Hallelujah?" It said do you want to make a tribute to Whitney?

Do you remember when you first met her or heard her voice (sing) etc.? Well I collected my thoughts on her and it reminded when I was 7 years old and visited Florida alone, the song I wanna dance with somebody stood out for me and it reminded me of the strength and courage I had received from it, well to be honest it was just that the video made me wanna dance and it made me happy at that moment, it helped to chase my fears and my kiddie blues away! It also caused me to think about my aunt in Florida who helped to raise me, who introduced and greatly instilled in me the knowledge of God in the first place, she even got me my first Bible (My Little Book Of Bible Stories) now my auntie is up in age so since I don't get to talk to her much, I was surprised and happy when I called last night and she answered, if you know what I mean, I'm not wishing no bad on her or anyone, but I'm just being realistic, but anyway we talked, laughed, reminisced, and all, God knows how I needed that. And when I hung up from with her I went into the other room to prepare a written tribute in Whitney's honor, now God knows the truth about me so I cannot tell a lie, at first I thought about here is my chance to get noticed more, because I write intriguing poetry and books mind you, but my marketing sucks, but here was another opportunity to me. I began writing and I got through the first part just fine, but when I start writing the poem, I kept getting stuck (writer's block) so with trust I had to take it to God, and ask if it's His will, because beside me trying to get noticed, I also wanted to do this for Whitney and her family, and for the most give God the glory . . . .

A Poem From The Heart

Whitney Houston an angel face with an angelic voice, you were specially selected as God's choice;

A woman so unique so pure so genuwine, who soared like an eagle and was a certain devine;

Everything does happen for a reason for me and for you, I will always love you and that stands to be true;

But just as I love you God loves you best, being at peace with Him and in Him you shall rest;

No matter what they think no matter what they say, you my dear Whitney always blew me away;

Your presence is what we needed a dose of reality, your pleasant smile and authentic personality;

As pretty as a flower and as sweet as a dove, sent nonstop straight from heaven above;

Thanking God for His gift He gave through you, Whitney Houston we love and will surely miss you . . . .

Rest in God and certainly rest in peace!!!

I wrote this poem last night (02-16-12) before I went to sleep, and when I did dream I dreamt of prophetic things, all around, but to me I was just dreaming, so when I woke up this morning, as any other morning, I say to myself, purpose, and after I do my morning prayer God's presence shows up and the revelation begins, and today it just happens to be about Whitney or at least surrounding her and her significance in my life. You gotta stay with me, it gets deeper and deeper, remember when I said God works in mysterious ways, as we all should know, but last night when I wrote the tribute, and today, this morning it has even more significance to me, allow me to explain; You know how in her song she says I wanna dance with somebody? Well God allowed me to see that the person to dance with is Jesus, and how she says when the night falls my lonely heart calls, well saints when you can't sleep at night and your spirit is troubled what do we do? We call upon the Lord, right? We need comfort, and wheew, when He comes in and sweeps us off our feet, we can dance dance dance all night, lol, well anyway God lead me to the song and why I recalled this song first in particular, yeah I wanna dance with somebody, with somebody who loves me, (doesn't Jesus love us)?

God also caused me to recall the Cinderella story I had watched the other night with Whitney Houston and Brandi, and how I am rewriting the stageplay, rather working on this particular project and renaming it The Magnificent Ball (Cinderella the Saint), I can feel God all over this, and as I said and know not all will believe, but to those who do, watch out now! The other songs that stands out to me in my spirit are: I believe in miracles, One moment in time, Greatest Love of All (Jesus), and We got something in common (we both love the Lord and crazy about Him), I wanna run to you (I wanna run to You Jesus), I look to you, Count on me and I love the Lord, I'm really loving this tribute to Whitney on WIDU 1600 AM, its really enlightening me more on Whitney's spiritual relationship with God, and it is God who is leading me to this, because it causes me to gain even more inspiration in Him, Amen . . . .

Its not over

Just when I thought I was done with the whole Whitney Houston discussion, tribute, and all, as I sit here and watch The Talk, and they're talking with Kevin, and theres more, as he quotes that there are some that wonders what would make a woman of her status and so young feel so down that would do something so catastrophic and cause her own death, and a lot of people are speculating and assuming what might have happened, and the only person that can answer for certain is God, they're debating on her honorary, well, you better believe that the honor goes to God, but being fair they should accommodate her family with justification as necessary, they need to look at her outstanding effectiveness she has had on the town and it's people and this nation and all, look at how she was loved not only as a great performer but as a person too, yes she may have had drug problems and whatever else, but now who does not have a personal life?, and it might not be so pleasant to all, as I was always taught you can't please everybody, and in her defense, yes I'm saved and I'm trying my best to be as pleasant at all times to everyone, but there will be someone in the crowd to at least tempt you if not succeed in pushing you off your square and taking you off your focus, that's why we have to depend on God daily for strength, but anyway, you will not always feel so great, especially if you're struggling with something (demons)they're trying to focus the attention on her incident of when she had the issue at the party prior to her death, I was diagnosed with bipolar years ago and that reminded me of myself, at times I would be so happy and sweet with and to people, strangers and all, but when irked, I would suddenly change and snap, sorta like Dr. Jeckel and Mr. Hide, and yes it is demonic, but praise God I am more focused to deal with it, like I said I still have some episodes, but the more I stay focused on God the better I can deal with it, we stand in the way of the accuser so he will do all he can to make that happen that we may be accused (falsely I might add) but God, can turn that around, Amen? So no matter what they say, Whitney I know what God allowed you to do for me, so I look pass that and I urge all to do the same, lets not judge others, Amen?

This is a post from Facebook; 2 Corinthians 12:7; And lest I should be exalted above measure through the abundance of the revelations, there was given to me a thorn in the flesh, the messenger of satan to buffet me, lest I should be exalted above measure. "Make me weak so you can be strong Jesus", We all want the thorns removed from our beautiful rose but God allows some thorns to remain for others to warn them to handle us with care & remember it is God working through us and not ourselves, and for us to always remain humble in the abundance of revelation & responsibility, lest we become vain, for when we are weak He is strong!!!

I feel strongly that God wants His people (all people) to know that there is tremendous hope in Him, its not time to give up, its far from over when you trust in Him, in fact I can testify that its just the beginning, Amen?

But don't give up, but give in to God, and He will give you peace, He'll give you joy and happiness, He indeed will give you your heart's desires, He said so in His word. I have been lead by the guidance of God to come to you and present this message to you in my own unique way, but I know you see His hand all over this, I have true confidence in the Lord, and just as this is a true state of urgency, time is of the essence and not worth wasting, theres no time like the present, and the time is now that you seek God, as I always say, do your best and let God do the rest, He can do anything but fail, Amen???

The Moment Of Truth is a unique design with the intent to target people of all walks of life, to plant your focus on our creator, the one who loves us, the one who will provide for us, the one who we can definitely take refuge in, (Psalms 46:1 says; God is our refuge and strength, a very help in present trouble. And He will bless us all in all, should we trust in Him. And I strongly emphasize that you don't have to be perfect for Him to love you, but only if you try, and I also would like to say without scorn and conviction, but with desperation out of love, don't let it be said too late, Amen . . . .

Compassionate

What would Jesus do? Is the question most asks, well He set examples in every situation through His healing, His love, when He fed the people and all, but that content and intent seems to be far from this generation, where is the love? I pass people in grocery stores, in the public, even in the church, and I speak to folks and they look at me so strange, they dare not to speak back and they act like I stole their teeth, because half the time they refuse to even smile. I ask myself what is wrong with the people, this world is so ruined with hatred, if they're not hating you they're hating on you, and for no reason at all, I always say this, if you're happy with yourself and what God has done and is doing for you there would be no room for hating on someone else. Oh and what about the rude treatment to the special needs people? I am so glad that God has worked with me in so many areas and changed my mind on how I thought about some people and issues and people with the issues; my experience has taught me to show more compassion toward the people, even when they don't want it, but God knows whats best, Amen? I fell in love with this scripture once I figured it out and learned it;

Exodus 4: 10-11; 10. And Moses said unto the Lord, O my Lord, I am not eloquent, neither heretofore, nor since thou hast spoken unto thy servant: but I am slow of speech, and of a slow tongue. 11. And the Lord said unto him, who hath made man's mouth? Or the seeing or the blind? Have not I the Lord?

"I am certainly glad that I had my dose of reality and snapped out of it, and am no longer a respecter of persons, I admit I was just that dumbfounded at a point, but thank God for His mercy, He changed me around, Amen!!!

Who will you serve?

God is so peculiar, questionable, marvelous, strange, but of course I mean that in a good way, because He does strange things in strange ways, things you don't really even think of or imagine, that's why He says He can do things and give us exceedingly above all we can think or ask, (we can't even imagine the surprises that God pops on us) Amen? But I truly thank Him for wisdom and insight, and lining things up for me, now this may be even strange to some of you, but do pay close attention;

Yesterday Sunday worship was a little odd, a bit different in a sense, because I'm always sincerely seeking Him and praising Him, but yesterday something had taken place right before service began, plus my mom being absent was heavy on my heart, I was troubled, but when we did devotion (prayer)as usual, He answered me with a song, and that song sang by the choir was everything is gonna be alright, "aw man, I felt that so strongly in my spirit, God was speaking to me and reassuring me through the song, remember this about me, I say we need to pay close attention to all things around us God speaks through all things (song, numbers, other people, etc) anyhow the message was about seeking God first, which was the same message given at Whitney Houston's funeral, well I don't see it as cliché', but as God does, He chooses the same message to go through and be presented by several people (in fact as many as He wants) but its clear to me that theres a message that He want the people to hear and get, "so pastor preach on". When I got home I was lead to read 1 Kings 18: 21-39, and it reads;

And E-li'-jah came unto all the people, and said. How long halt the between two opinions? If the Lord be God, follow Him: but if Ba'-al, then follow him. And the people answered him not a word. 22. Then E-li'-jah unto the people, I, even I only, remain a prophet of the Lord; but Ba'-al's prophets are four hundred and fifty men. 23. Let them therefore give us two bullocks; and let them choose one bullock for themselves, and cut it in pieces, and lay it on wood, and put no fire under: 24. And call on the name of your gods, and I will call on the name of the Lord: and the God that answereth by fire, let Him be God. And all the people answered and said, It is well spoken. 25. And E-li'-jah said unto the prophets of Ba'-al, choose you one bullock for yourselves, and dress it first; for ye are many; and call on the name of your gods, but put no fire under. 26. And they took the bullock which was given them, and they dressed it, and they called on the name o Ba'-al from morning even until noon, saying, O Ba'-al, hear us, But there was no voice, nor any that answered. And they leaped upon the alter which was made. 27. And it came to pass at noon, that E-li'-jah mocked them, and said, Cry aloud : for he is a god; either he is talking, or he is persuing, or he is in a journey, or peradventure he sleepeth, and must be awaked.

28. And they cried aloud, and cut themselves after their manner with knives and lancets, till the blood gushed out upon them. 29. And it came to pass, when midday was past, and they prophesied until the time of the offering of the evening sacrifice, that there was neither voice nor any to answer, nor any that regarded.30. And E-li'-jah said until all the people, Come near unto me. And all the people came near unto him. And he repaired the altar of the Lord that was broken down. 31. And E-li'-jah took twelve stones, according to the number of the number of the tribes of the sons of Jacob, unto who the word of the Lord came, saying, Israel shall be thy name: 32. And with the stones he built an altar in the name of the Lord: and he made a trench about the altar, as great as would contain two measures of seed.33. And he put the wood in order, and cut the bullock in pieces, and laid him on the wood, and said, Fill four barrels with water, and pour it on the burnt sacrifice, and on the wood. 34. And he said do it the second time. And they did it the second time. And he said do it the third time. And they did it the third time. 35. And the water ran round about the altar; and he filled the trench also with water. 36. And it came to pass at the time of the offering of the evening sacrifice, that E-li'-jah the prophet came near, and said, Lord God of Abraham, Isaac, and of Israel let it be known this day that thou art God in Israel, and that I am thy servant, and I have done all these things at thy word. 37. Hear me, O Lord, hear me, that this people may know that thou art the Lord God, and that thou hast turned their heart back again. 38. Then the fire of the Lord

fell, and consumed the burnt sacrifice, and the wood, and the stones, and the dust, and licked up the water that was in the trench. 39. And when all the people saw it, they fell on their faces: and they said, The Lord, he is God; the Lord, he is the God. 40. And E-li'-jah said unto them, Take the prophets of Ba'-al; let not one of them escape. And they took them: and E-li'-jah brought them down to the brook and slew them there. People people people we have to be careful of what we say and choose, there is only one God, and yes Jesus is the way! And you see how he sent E-li'-jah to kill the prophets of Ba'-al? Theres danger when you go the wrong way and serve the wrong gods, like when I was in the nail shop the other day getting my nails done, and the technician doing my nails the Holy Spirit lead me to ask her if she went to church (which in hindsight I guess I knew the obvious) but like I said the Spirit lead me and we all know or should know that when God wants you or tell you to do something, you had better obey, plus His understanding is far more intelligent than our's, (whats foolish to men is wisdom of God, Amen) anyway she answered no, with an added,

"I have a religion that's a bhudda", I paused and answered, "I figured that", and then a moment later I followed up with more questions about bhudda, which I'm familiar, but once again I had to follow my leading, and after a couple of questions, she looks over to her dad or whoever he was (an older Chinese man of course) and she say ask him, which he was already looking over and ready to jump in on the conversation, and here it got more interesting, when he said to me if you wanna know about bhudda look on the internet, well I asked him would he rather I get my info from the net, that could be saying anything about his god, or would he rather testify about the things he did for him and through him, well he just got agitated and kept telling me to look on Google, wow I thought because I can testify and what convinces me more is my experiences what the Lord has done for me and through me, so I can proudly say that my God is alive, but I was saddened for her, because if you don't really know about what you're following or what you're trusting in and praising, wouldn't that scare you? She actually had to trust in someone else to explain for her, either that or she was just afraid to discuss it with him present (I don't know if they'll be tortured or beat or something) but thank God theres no punishment for talking about Jesus, only gifts and blessings, Amen? Anyway the lady who's nails he was doing jumped in confessing and testifying, so that gave me some reassurance to know that I got back up, lol, but you know how you pray and ask God to give you the words to say and who to say them to and where to go, its really amazing if you let God line things up for you, but anyway He lined it all up for me, I didn't know that there would be another saint in the midst, and someone who can quote scriptures with me in agreement, and when I was long done with my nails, and was in another part of the salon I still heard the man and the woman (bhuddist and Christian) debating and discussing things, so I thought, "thank you Lord', because maybe this was something (a work) You wanted done by others, but you used me to open the doors to the conversation, Amen! "I really love the Lord", and I know that He loves me . . . .

Random Thoughts

God loves you, He wants you to be happy and successful! Success comes in the form of wealth/financial, health, emotional, personal, and more;

He wants you to be your best, and as a witness when you trust in Him you will be just that. I personally had a lot of growing to do and I am yet still growing in Him, I've found love, happiness, strength, stability, all that I did not have when I was alone in the dark (basically living my life and not focusing on God) now this is not intended for everyone, just like the word of God, everyone will not get it or understand it or even believe and trust in it, but to those that God has purpose for and those who love God and want more, this just might be what you need and been waiting for, Amen? God understands that we are not perfect nor do we live in a perfect world but through God its possible, it may not always be easy but its possible, you just need the desire, the will, and the strength, and by God the go ahead/green light . . . .

This has been a delightful experience for me to bring to you my authentic details and input on Devine involvement, and in my own words (causing it to be unique) this is also a self—help product, for I encourage you to get yourself and your house in order, as the word says 1 Timothy 2:4 Who will have all men to be saved, and to come unto the knowledge of the truth. (Desires to), and again I urge you to not let it be said too late, this is The Moment Of Truth and it is upon us, so what are we gonna do about it? I mean I hear all this stuff about the different dates that the world is supposed to end, its really silly to me that a person can think that if he saved some tuna, bread, water, flashlights, etc. that he would be safe, first of all if the end was to come, what are you gonna do with that stuff in heaven, and if it's the end, then how could you use any of it if it's the end, the last time I checked the end means that's it, it's a wrap, its over, etc. Its just messed up how we will believe man's word over God's, we are too gullible but the word of God says that His people must not worry, I strongly feel that's why we fast to prepare our spiritual bodies to be without food, but even God provided the people in the wilderness the manna (which is what I was taught the angels did eat). Don't you wanna feel safe too?

Let Us Pray

A prayer for the lost: "Dear God I believe that you exist but I'm not sure how to find my way to you or back to you, but I want your love I want your trust, I want to trust in you, I want to live sin free, I don't want my soul to go to hell, I have tried many of things and I couldn't be helped but I am told that you can help me so I wanna be happy, I want to be able to love more, so help me God, Amen!

A prayer for the confused: "Dear God I want to believe in You but I'm not sure about you, I don't know what to believe, as you know there are so many different teachings and religions in this world and I don't want to be confused, so God help me to follow the right path, help me to learn more about you, and teach me to pray how you want me to pray to you, Amen!

A prayer for the children: "Dear God thank you for all that you done for me, keep me good, teach me to be better, and teach me to please you, Amen!

A prayer for the saints: "Father God, thank you for blessing me by sending your anointed Holy Spirit to dwell with me, it has been the comforter that you promised, it has been the strength that I needed, it provides the comfort I seek, I am so happy and glad that you trusted me with your gift, Heavenly Father I want to be all that I can be for you and may I be acceptable in your sight, keep me O Lord, you are in control of my destiny and I trust you to make that a perfect completion, I thank you and I love you, Amen!

Epilogue

I just wanna say in closing, I got me some hand clapping, feet stomping revelations even for myself, I can feel the excitement, I wish the same for you, and together lets look to the Lord and forward to Him extremely blessing us! The Moment Of Truth was a project that has been on my mind for some time but in different concepts, ideas, and approaches/plans, but I had to let God show me how He wanted me to do this and let Him bring it forth in His own timing, especially since I decided to wait on Him and trust in Him!

But I'm grateful that He chose me and trusted me to do this assignment, I was about to say project again, and which I had in the past, but God showed me that a project is something that takes building and planning, but an assignment is already put together and ordained, "thank you Lord for ordaining this". Again, I touch and agree with those that believe and I stand in the gap for those who don't and those struggling with doing so.